Poet's England ~1

BUCKINGHAMSHIRE

BERKSHIRE

OXFORDSHIRE

compiled by Margaret Tims

line drawings by Gillian Durrant

BRENTHAM PRESS
London W5

i

Foreword

POET'S ENGLAND does not set out with this first
volume to become a definitive anthology of English
'regional' verse.   The intention rather is to
present an evocation of the 'spirit of the place'
(and its people) through a variety of moods and
interpretations.   It is selective rather than
comprehensive, seeking a balance between the old
and the new; between the landscape of topography
and the landscape of heart and mind; between the
lettered and the unlettered, the formal and the
spontaneous.   In the interests of this balance,
it has been necessary to adopt the otherwise
regrettable practice of using only extracts from
a number of longer works.

The poets are not confined to the great names of
English literature, although the great ones
naturally appear.   The criterion of selection
has been truth to a vision or a mood, and this
may run through all levels of literature.   So
alongside the classics of Spenser and Chaucer,
Pope and Gray, or Keats and Shelley, may be read
the labourer, the shoemaker and the gardener.
In our own day, contributors to this volume
include a schoolboy and members of a women's
institute, together with more professional verse-
turners and not omitting the Poet Laureate.

Buckinghamshire, Berkshire and Oxfordshire
embraces that area of southern England broadly
known as 'Thames and Chilterns', although neither
fits entirely within the region.   Recent changes
in county boundaries have presented problems.
We have preferred to keep the traditional Downs
and White Horse in Berks, together with Abingdon
and Appleton, though Oxon can now claim all of
these.   Nor have we transplanted Burnham Beeches
from Bucks to Berks, as county arboriculturists
direct.

Acknowledgments

For access to local collections and other helpful
information thanks are due to the County Library,
Aylesbury; City Reference Library, Reading; Central
Library, Oxford; Central Reference Library, Ealing;
and to the Arts Council Poetry Library.

I am indebted to Sir John Betjeman for his unpub-
lished lines written for Wing Airport resistance
movement and to Philip Pacey for his unpublished
poem 'Charged Landscape, Uffington'. To Maurice
Bond for his translation of 'Hymn of Master John
Schorn' *(Records of Bucks, 15, V, 1951)*; Stanley
Brandon for 'Hardwicke' from *Ventures in Verse by
Children* (ed. E Beatrice Cheyne, 1952); Dr C. K.
Coles for 'Banbury Cross' by Arthur MacDonald from
Sportive Ditties (Aylesbury, c.1930); Mr R. C.
Howard for 'The Year Passes' by H Evelyn Howard
from *At the Sign of the Swan* (Chesham, 1937);
Mrs G. H. Blanchett for 'Thoughts on the Hill above
Islip Bridge' and Mrs M. Gallie for 'Ode to the
Monthly Meeting' by Grace Henman, both from *Poems
from Islip W.I.* (1954); *Slough Observer* for 'Come
Back, Sir John!' by John Jones (1971); Maida
Stanier for 'Freshmen' from *The New Oxford Spy*
(Blackwell, 1969); Miss Alice G. Wright for 'The
Pancake Bell' by Thomas Wright from *Bucks and
Northants Ballads* (Olney, 1925).
Acknowledgement is given to: Miss D. E. Collins
and Eyre Methuen Ltd for part of 'The Ballad of the
White Horse' by G. K. Chesterton from *Collected
Poems* (1927); J.M. Dent & Sons Ltd for part of
'Alma Mater' by Sir Arthur Quiller-Couch from *The
Vigil of Venus* (1912); Macmillan London and
Basingstoke for 'Cowper at Olney' by Sylvia Lynd
from *Collected Poems* (1945); John Murray for part
of 'Slough' and 'Upper Lambourne' by John Betjeman
from *Collected Poems* (1958); A. D. Peters & Co Ltd
for part of 'Can This be Oxford?' by Hilaire Belloc
from *Sonnets and Verse* (1938); Martin Secker &
Warburg Ltd for 'In Burnham Beeches' and 'At Oxford'
by Andrew Young from *Complete Poems,* ed Leonard
Clark (1960); The Society of Authors, represent-
ing the estate of John Masefield, for part of
'Reynard the Fox' and 'Lollington Downs'.
The following sources are also acknowledged: 'King
Charles I' by Hugh Chesterman from *Kings and Other
Things* (Methuen, 1930); 'Buckinghamshire' by Eva
N. Rolls (*Chiltern Life,* January 1972); 'Bucking-
hamshire Place Names' by Theodora Roscoe (Bucks

Poetry Society Collection, 1941); 'My Home in Bucks' by W. T. Thorpe (copy in possession of Bucks County Library); 'The Little Hills' by Cartwright Timms (*Chiltern Life,* March/April, 1972). Illustration of Huntley & Palmer's factory at Reading by courtesy of Associated Biscuits Ltd;and drawing of Slough by courtesy of Slough Borough Council.

February 1976   M.T.

New boundaries _____

Old boundaries ....

Contents

Oxfordshire

Buckinghamshire

MY HOME IN BUCKS

Choicest of smaller counties of this isle.
Well planned, the sons of nature to beguile,
With beechy woodlands mingling downy lawns
Like opals set in ever changing dawns.
My county! watered by the Thame and Ouse,
With limpid Chess to tempt the poet's muse,
Or lave the feet of Chilterns, many hilled
In heaving waves by petrifaction stilled.
Fair Bucks! scion of Eden richly dowered
With copious orchards in profusion showered,
Thy russet farmsteads vested green and gold
Are but the emblems of great wealth untold.

'Tis here my home I make, and freely breathe,
As with the battle won, my sword I sheathe;
Blest in this shire by history enshrined
With names of many of man's noblest kind.
My walls are built with memories replete
As make my home a "Chequers" for retreat.
My garden walks are paced by shades of men
Like Milton, Hampden, Beaconsfield and Penn,
Whose travails made it possible to be
Resigned to this more peaceful liberty.
And here I wing my soul with finer plume
In ready poise for flight to ampler room.

W.T. Thorpe

BUCKINGHAMSHIRE

How can I tell the beauty of this county,
Or recount the treasure of her bounty?
How beautiful the beechwoods, gently shaded,
Which in the Spring are thickly bluebell gladed!
Beneath the new grown leaves of softest green
The little song-birds sweetly sing unseen.

Covering the Chilterns, fields and meadows lay
Hedged about by sapling and sweet May.
And in the Autumn, look like cloth of gold
Upon those hills, which never can grow old.
Even in the Winter, white with frost and snow,
We see them still in sombre beauty glow.

Beside a road, where ceaseless traffic streams,
Stands Milton's Cottage, where he wrote his dreams.
A simple house, so quiet and serene,
Yet many go and look upon this scene;
Some there are, who only stand and stare,
But some recall the poems written there.

And there beneath High Wycombe's highest hill
Lie caves, where men once tried the devil's skill.
Was it in earnest, or was it done in jest,
They wished to put their evil to the test?
But now the caves are only kept for show,
A tourist place, where people like to go.

Where is the place of peacefulness and rest?
It is Jordans, that sweet vale so blest,
Where Friends in their meeting house of prayer
Seek and worship God, their Father, there.
And from the city's maddening toil and strife
Men, for a moment, find a calmer life.

When Autumn paints the leaves of Burnham Beeches
Far and wide their fame of glory reaches,
Of Whiteleaf woods the tale is also told
With all their shades of copper and of gold.
And as we stand in awe beneath the trees,
We know that only God created these.

Between its banks, the River Chess does flow,
Past Chalfont, Latimer and Chenies it will go.
And as I wander on, with calm contented mind,
Such beauty thus in Buckinghamshire I find.
Surely in these scenes so lovely, rich and rare,
She can with all of England still compare.

Eva N. Rolls

BUCKINGHAMSHIRE PLACE NAMES

So take the Upper Icknield Way
Through Wendover and roam
Across the Chilterns to the woods
Of Hampden's ancient home.

There's Stokenchurch and Stewkley,
High Wycombe, Slough and Penn,
Stoke Mandeville; and Fingest,
Beech hidden in a glen.

There's Amersham and Aylesbury
And Beaconsfield, Coleshill,
There's Burnham, Wing; and Olney
Where lace is made with skill.

Between the Chalfonts, Peter, Giles,
And on past Shardeloes,
The Little Misbourne winds and curves,
From Missenden it flows.

On Bledlow Ridge the wind blows sweet
Across the Vale to Brill;
And guarding Hughenden there stands
The common of Naphill.

Theodora Roscoe

IN BURNHAM BEECHES

Walking among these smooth beech-boles
    With cracks and galls
And beetle-holes
    And ivy trickling in green waterfalls,

I noted carvings on their barks
    Faint and diffuse
As china marks
    On Worcester or old Bow: I wondered whose,

I feared that time had played its part
    With those whose token
Was a twin heart,
    So many hearts the swelling bark had broken.

Andrew Young

THE YEAR PASSES

Now winter scowls as Whyteleafe runs
In channels after winter rain
And the long blue Chiltern ribbon flings
Its coils across the Aylesbury plain.

Now spring is broken and the Chess
At Chenies stirs from sleep.   Ah, then
The water's pure and holy at
The spring at Little Missenden.

Now summer laughs on Hampden ferns
And honeysuckle.   Under Brill
The fields lie open to the sun
- And Olney Ouse is running still.

Now comes the glory of the woods
Out Aston way.   Their colours go,
A clean-cut passage, through my heart.
Now beacons glint at Ivinghoe.

Throughout the year old Grimsdyke runs
Throughout the year the box, the yew,
The Bledlow Ridge stand stiff and firm
And Penn, where Quakers lived and grew.

Throughout the year my passion goes;
By bluebells, poppies, beech-leaves fanned,
Thrown careless, to the chosen few
For only those who understand.

H. Evelyn Howard

from
ELEGY WRITTEN IN A COUNTRY CHURCH-YARD
[Stoke Poges]

The curfew tolls the knell of parting day,
The lowing herd winds slowly o'er the lea,
The plowman homeward plods his weary way,
And leaves the world to darkness and to me.

Now fades the glimmering landscape on the sight,
And all the air a solemn stillness holds,
Save where the beetle wheels his droning flight,
And drowsy tinklings lull the distant folds;

Save that from yonder ivy-mantl'd tow'r
The moping owl does to the moon complain
Of such, as wand'ring near her secret bow'r,
Molest her ancient solitary reign.

Beneath those rugged elms, that yew-tree's shade,
Where heaves the turf in many a mould'ring heap,
Each in his narrow cell for ever laid,
The rude Forefathers of the hamlet sleep.

The breezy call of incense-breathing Morn,
The swallow twitt'ring from the straw-built shed,
The cock's shrill clarion, or the echoing horn,
No more shall rouse them from their lowly bed.

For them no more the blazing hearth shall burn,
Or busy housewife ply her evening care:
No children run to lisp their sire's return,
Or climb his knees the envied kiss to share.

Oft did the harvest to their sickle yield,
Their furrow oft the stubborn glebe has broke;
How jocund did they drive their team afield!
How bow'd the woods beneath their sturdy stroke!

Let not Ambition mock their useful toil,
Their homely joys, and destiny obscure;
Nor Grandeur hear with a disdainful smile,
The short and simple annals of the poor.

The boast of heraldry, the pomp of pow'r,
And all that beauty, all that wealth e'er gave,
Awaits alike th' inevitable hour.
The paths of glory lead but to the grave.

Thomas Gray

THE LITTLE HILLS

These are the little hills, the quiet hills
Where peace abides.   The old and brooding trees
Scatter the shadows of high noon.   Time fills
An endless afternoon with endless hours
For clocks stand still.   Only a languid breeze
Ventures to stir beneath the poplar's towers.
Around these little hills the Meadow Brown
Flutters within the hawthorn's friendly shade.
The bindweed blossoms and the thistledown
Is wafted to green fields.   The skylark sings
Over a million grasses, every blade
Quivering as he mounts on tremulous wings.

This is the haunt of kestrel and of wren,
Where greenfinch twitters in the midday heat,
The linnet chatters in the gorse and then
Takes scurrying flight.   The grasshopper will play
Hie one-note fiddle in the fragrant sweet
Summer grass.   His song will last all day.
The little hills are still when twilight falls
And white moths flicker to the scented yield
Of meadowsweet.   A wakeful blackbird calls
From a crowded thorn.   And soon the first star gleam
Over the silent valley, over field,
Over the sleeping earth, that quietly dreams.

Cartwright Timms

from

REYNARD THE FOX

On old Cold Crendon's windy tops
Grows wintrily Blown Hilcote Copse,
Wind-bitten beech with badger barrows,
Where brocks eat wasp-grubs with their marrows,
And foxes lie on short-grassed turf,
Nose between paws, to hear the surf
Of wind in the beeches drowsily.
There was our fox bred lustily
Three years before, and there he berthed,
Under the beech-roots snugly earthed,
With a roof of flint and a floor of chalk
And ten bitten hens' heads each on its stalk,
Some rabbits' paws, some fur from scuts,
A badger's corpse and a smell of guts.

John Masefield

from
WOODLAND ECHOES

*[Poetical sketches of the scenery and objects
in that highly picturesque Vale through which
the Thames flows from Medmenham Abbey to Cliefden]*

From Hurley to green Hedsor's tow'rs
    The prospect winds with blending touch,
    To where, pavilion'd in its couch
Of dark alcoves and faded bow'rs,
The form of blighted Cliefden low'rs.
Below expand the shining fields,
Whose ever-teeming blossom yields
Rich treasure from the fertile soil,
To crown dull labor's drowsy toil.
A gentle distance from the place
Of Seymour's home, the eye may trace
The features of another scene,
    Where undulating valleys sweep
Their verdant swelling lines between
    The woods and hills, that crown each steep
    Which hangs above the delving deep.
Now, far along the leafy shades,
    The winding paths delightful lead,
To where the common's op'ning glades
    Sparkle with flocks and herds that feed
In quiet there, and, shining, throng
In many a snowy line along.
They start not at the sportive sounds
    The peasant boy in freedom chaunts,
But gambol in responsive rounds,
    And frolic in their noon-tide haunts.
There, in the furze, whose fadeless bloom
    Glitters upon its rugged breast,
The linnet seeks a secret home,
    To build security a nest.

William Tyler

from
THE VALE OF WYCOMBE

Delightful valley! whose luxurious meads
Crown'd with rich herbage floating to the breeze,
Enamell'd with the softest, gayest blooms,
By nature's lib'ral land profusely spread;
And on each side the graceful hills arise,
Whose crops abundant clothe the fertile soil,
And promise to the peasant rich reward,
Striving to vie with the prolific vale.
Nor less the sylvan scenes their charms display,
Whose widespread foliage forms the cooling shade,
And sooths the languors of the fervid noon.
While down below Wick's fair, meand'ring stream,
Betwixt the bending willows steals along;
But soon arrested in her calm career,
Th' obstructing dam demands a transient pause;
She's then conducted to the torturing wheel,
Whose horrid crash thro' all the valley sounds!
Then quits with rapid flight the tyrant's paw;
But when to safer distance far arriv'd,
Her agitated breast becomes compos'd,
And as she roves along the sandy bed
Her injuries in softest murmurs tells.

But cease thy mournful murmurings, thou'lt soon
Be freed from toil and torture: Father Thames
Will close enfold thee in his fond embrace,
And thy kind guardian and protector prove;
With him in nobler service then engag'd,
To Britain's shores shall thy soft bosom bear
The *wealth* and *worth* of every distant clime.

William Lane

from
GENIUS OF THE THAMES

Delight shall check th' expanded sail
In woody Marlow's winding vale:
And fond regret for scenes so fair
With backward gaze shall linger there,
Till rise romantic Hedsor's hills,
And Cliefden's groves, and springs, and rills.

Thomas Love Peacock

from
THE REVOLT OF ISLAM

*[written at Marlow and dedicated to
Mary Shelley]*

The toil which stole from thee so many an hour,
Is ended, - and the fruit is at thy feet!
No longer where the woods to frame a bower
With interlacéd branches mix and meet,
Or where with sound like many voices sweet,
Waterfalls leap among wild islands green,
Which framed for my lone boat a lone retreat
Of moss-grown trees and weeds, shall I be seen:
But beside thee, where still my heart has ever been.

Percy Bysshe Shelley

HARDWICKE

As you walk along in town, under the hot sun,
And cannot see the trees in their lovely green coats;
When you look around you and see houses and motors
You would rather be in the country
Where the birds are flying among the trees
And the bees are gathering their honey
Little rabbits are running about, in and out
Of their holes by the hedges;
In a little while, as you walk along by the pond,
A moorhen rises and flies before you.

As the clouds sail along in the bright air
They are like flocks of sheep roaming in wide
    blue fields;
And the birds are pleased that they have their
    young ones,
They are singing happily:
All the pretty trees are blooming,
Their blossoms look like snow powdered over the
    branches:
The swallows have come back from sunny lands.

Walking up to the top of the hill,
Catching every breath of air as you go along,
You will see in the distance the blue hills of
    Wendover
And nearer are spread the cornfields, shining like
    gold
Under the rays of the great yellow sun:
Nearer still are the hayfields
Where the farmers are leading their loads to the
    rickyards.

Looking down on the other side
You see the brook winding away
Among the reeds and willow trees;
Beyond it stands the Church, old and grey,
Above all the red-roofed houses,
Its tower seeming to reach the sky
As if leading upward all their prayers
Or perhaps it is their thanks they offer
For the peace and wonder of this countryside.

                              Stanley Brandon
                              [aged twelve]

from
POLY-OLBION

For Aylesbury's vale that walloweth in her wealth
And (by her wholesome air continually in health)
Is lusty, firm, and fat, and holds her youthful
   strength.

                         Michael Drayton

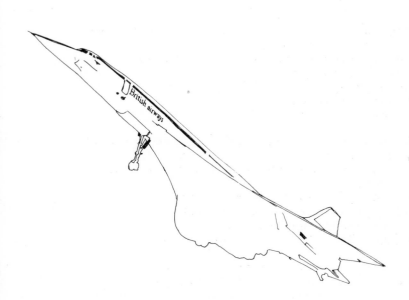

WING AIRPORT RESISTANCE MOVEMENT
[lines read at protest meeting, June 1970]

The birds are all killed and the flowers are all dead,
And the businessman's aeroplane booms overhead,
With chemical sprays we have poisoned the soil
And the scent in our nostrils is diesel and oil.

The roads are all widened, the lanes are all straight,
So that rising executives won't have to wait,
For who'd use a footpath to Quainton or Brill,
When a jet can convey you so fast to Brazil?

                         John Betjeman

KING CHARLES THE FIRST

King Charles the First to Parliament came,
Five good Parliament men to claim;
King Charles he had them each by name,
Denzyl Holles and Jonathan Pym,
And William Strode and after him,
Arthur Hazelrigg Esquire
And Hampden, Gent, of Buckinghamshire.

The man at the gate said "Tickets, please",
Said Charles, "I've come for the five MPs".
The porter said "Which?" and Charles said
    "These:
Denzyl Holles and Jonathan Pym,
And William Strode and after him,
Arthur Hazelrigg Esquire
And Hampden, Gent, of Buckinghamshire."

In at the great front door he went,
The great front door of Parliament,
While, out at the back with one consent
Went Denzyl Holles and Jonathan Pym,
And William Strode and after him,
Arthur Hazelrigg Esquire
And Hampden, Gent, of Buckinghamshire.

Into the street strode Charles the First,
His nose was high and his lips were pursed,
While, laugh till their rebel sides near burst,
    did
Denzyl Holles and Jonathan Pym,
And William Strode and after him,
Arthur Hazelrigg Esquire
And Hampden, Gent, of Buckinghamshire.

                                    Hugh Chesterman

from
THE BUCKINGHAMSHIRE RAILWAY (1849)

To my kind readers:

The Author of this little work
    A Gardener has been;
Most of his lifetime has been spent
    'Mongst flowers and shrubs so green.

My age now more than sixty is,
    And work of late was short;
Thus for some other employment,
    To the pen I did resort.

First I wrote "The Beauties of Stowe",
    With very great success;
Then the Travels of our good Queen,
    Indeed they were no less.

And something new this winter did
    Across my mind prevail,
To describe the wond'rous benefits
    Derived from Steam and Rail.

The Cuttings and Embankments all,
    On this, the great Bucks line;
The Bridges and the Viaducts
    Of masonry so fine.

The advantages of travelling,
    And great contrast between
The old stage coach, and post-horses,
    As on the rail is seen.

And if this meets encouragement,
    Which is my expectation,
I'll try and full description give
    Of Wolverton's Grand Station.

              Charles Whitehall

With Envy stung, and Emulation fired,
Nature and *Art*, each separately, aspired
To guide the Pleasures of th' admiring few
In Objects great, or beautiful, or new.
    Nature the Forest plants, extends the Plain,
Paints the blue Hill, and spreads the glassy Main:
Here lengthen'd Views allow the Eye to range;
More bounded Prospects there the Lanskip change.
Art bids;   and, lo! obedient Cities rise,
And glitt'ring Spires shoot upwards to the Skies:
It pompous Bulk the splendid Palace rears,
And each gay Order on its Front appears.
    Separate these Rivals thus aspire to fame,
But each, misguided, lost her purpos'd Aim.
All cry aloud, when *Nature*'s Works appear,
What vast Extravagance, what Wildness here!
Nor pleased with *Art* alone, each Eye can see
Stiffness in her, and trim Formality.
    Baffled in each Attempt, at Length they cease
Their fierce Dispute, and knit in Leagues of Peace;
Determined with associate Powers to shew
One matchless Effort of their Force at STOW.
    The World astonish'd, as the Labour grew,
Exclaims, "What cannot *Art* and *Nature* do!

B. Seeley

OF THE USE OF RICHES

[from Moral Essays, Epistle IV]

    Still follow Sense, of ev'ry Art the Soul,
Parts answ'ring parts shall slide into a whole,
Spontaneous beauties all around advance,
Start ev'n from Difficulty, strike from Chance;
Nature shall join you;   Time shall make it grow
A Work to wonder at - perhaps a STOWE.

Alexander Pope

e Ouse, slow winding through a level plain
 spacious meads with cattle sprinkled o'er,
ducts the eye along his sinuous course
lighted.   There, fast rooted in their bank,
and, never overlook'd, our fav'rite elms,
at screen the herdsman's solitary hut;
ile far beyond, and overthwart the stream
at, as with molten glass, inlays the vale,
e sloping land recedes into the clouds;
splaying on its varied side the grace
 hedge-row beauties numberless, square tow'r,
ll spire, from which the sound of cheerful bells
st undulates upon the list'ning ear,
oves, heaths, and smoking villages remote.
enes must be beautiful, which, daily view'd,
ease daily, and whose novelty survives
ng knowledge and the scrutiny of years.

William Cowper

se having Olney past, as she were waxed mad,
om her first staider course immediately doth gad,
d in meandering gyves doth whirl herself about
at, this way here and there, back, forwards, in and out;
d, like a wanton girl, oft doubting in her gait,
e labyrinth like turns and turnings intricate,
rough these rich fields doth run.

Michael Drayton

COWPER AT OLNEY

In this green valley where the Ouse
Is looped in many a silver pool,
Seeking God's mercy and his muse
Went Cowper sorrowful.

Like the pale gleam of wintry sun
His genius lit the obscure place,
Where, battling with despair, lived one
Of melancholy's race.

By quiet waters, by green fields
In winter sweet as summer hay,
By hedgerows where the chaffinch build
He went his brooding way.

And not a berry or a leaf,
Or stirring bough or fragrant wind,
But, in its moment, soothed the grief
Of his tormented mind.

And since, like the beloved sheep
Of David's shepherd, he was led
By streams and pastures quiet as sleep -
Was he not comforted?

Sylvia Lynd

from
THE PANCAKE BELL

At Olney when good Bess was queen
    The pancake bell was rung,
And sweeter sound ne'er scurried
    From steeple, crowde or tongue.

The girls when Robin touched the rope
    Their batter made, and by it
They stood, and at the first "Ting-tang"
    Began straightway to fry it.

The sizzling done, the sugar last
    They spread - sagacious people!
Then rushed with pan and pancake hot
    Pell-mell toward the steeple.

Ran one-and-twenty maids that morn,
    As documents discover,
But Ann was far the fleetest for
    The ringer was her lover.

                        T. Wright

[crowde: instrument resembling a violin]

HYMN OF MASTER JOHN SCHORN

[Rector of North Marston, 1290-1314]

Hail, gem of pastors,
O John, flower of teachers,
rector of Marston

Hail, light of preachers,
vessel of virtues, way of manners
leading to heaven

Hail, father of clerks
example of priests
in chastity of body

Hail, companion of angels,
who dost enjoy the heavens,
and conqueror of demons

Hail, help of the sick,
medicine of those harassed
by the pain of fevers

Hail, light of the eyes,
liberator of the weak
from the toothache

Hail, since the ox
restored to life
gives witness of your miracles

Hail, thou who art the
rescuer of all the drowned
by thy prayers

Hail, heavenly consoler
of wretched boys
who are in sadness

Hail, leader of pilgrims,
lead thou wayfarers
to the joys above.

Pray for us, John, priest of Christ
That the grace of Christ may defend us from all fever

[translated from original Lati
by Maurice Bond]

24

Berkshire

from
THE SEASONS
[Summer]

Slow let us trace the matchless vale of Thames;
Fair-winding up to where the muses haunt
In Twit'nam's bowers, and for their Pope implore
The healing god; to royal Hampton's pile,
To Clermont's terraced height, and Esher's groves,
Where in the sweetest solitude, embraced
By the soft windings of the silent Mole,
From courts and senates Pelham finds repose.
Enchanting vale! beyond whate'er the muse
Has of Achaia or Hesperia sung!
O vale of bliss! O softly-swelling hills!
On which the power of cultivation lies,
And joys to see the wonders of his toil.
   Heavens! what a goodly prospect spreads around,
Of hills, and dales, and woods, and lawns, and spires,
And glittering towns, and gilded streams, till all
The stretching landskip into smoke decays!

James Thomson

from
PROTHALAMION

There, in a Meadow, by the Rivers side,
A Flocke of *Nymphes* I chaunced to espy,
All lovely Daughters of the Flood thereby,
With goodly greenish locks all loose untyde,
As each had been a Bryde,
And each one had a little wicker basket,
Made of fine twigs entrayled curiously,
In which they gathered flowers to fill their flasket:
And with fine Fingers, cropped full feateously
The tender stalks on hye.
Of every sort, which in that Meadow grew,
They gathered some; the Violet pallid blew,
The little Dazie, that at evening closes,
The virgin Lillie, and the Primrose trew,
With store of vermeil Roses,
To decke their Bridegroomes posies,
Against the Brydale day, which was not long:
Sweet *Themmes* runne softly, till I end my Song.

With that, I saw two Swannes of goodly hewe,
Come softly swimming downe along the Lee;
Two fairer Birds I yet did never see:
The snow which doth the top of *Pindus* strew,
Did never whiter shew,
Nor *Jove* himselfe when he a Swan would be
For love of *Leda*, whiter did appeare:
Yet *Leda* was they say as white as he,
Yet not so white as these, nor nothing neare;
So purely white they were,
That even the gentle streame, the which them bare,
Seem'd foule to them, and bad his billowes spare
To wet their silken feathers, least they might
Soyle their fayre plumes with water not so fayre,
And marre their beauties bright,
That shone as heavens light,
Against their Brydale day, which was not long:
Sweete *Themmes* runne softly, till I end my Song.

Edmund Spenser

from
POLY-OLBION

But now this mighty flood, upon his voyage prest,
(That found how with his strength, his beauties still
   increased,
From where brave Windsor stood on tiptoe to behold
The fair and goodly Thames, so far as e'er he could,
With kingly houses crowned, of more than earthly pride,
Upon his either banks, as he along doth glide),
With wonderful delight doth his long course pursue,
Where Oatlands, Hampton Court, and Richmond he doth
   view.

Michael Drayton

from
WINDSOR FOREST

Here hills and vales, the woodland and the plain,
Here earth and water seem to strive again;
Not Chaos-like together crush'd and bruis'd,
But, as the world, harmoniously confus'd;
Where order in variety we see,
And where, tho' all things differ, we agree.

Here waving groves a chequer'd scene display,
And part admit, and part exclude the day;
As some coy nymph her lover's warm address
Nor quite indulges, nor can quite repress.
There, interspers'd in lawns and opening glades,
Thin trees arise, that shun each other's shades.
Here in full light the russet plains extend:
There wrapt in clouds the blueish hills ascend.

Ev'n the wild heath displays her purple dyes,
And 'midst the desert fruitful fields arise,
That crowned with tufted trees and springing corn
Like verdant isles the sable waste adorn.
Let India boast her plants, nor envy we
The weeping amber or the balmy tree,
While by our oaks the precious loads are born,
And realms commanded which those trees adorn.

Alexander Pope

WINDSOR CASTLE

Lines written by King James I of Scotland
during his imprisonment in the Round Tower,
1406 to 1423

Now was there made, fast by the touris wall,
A garden fair, - and in the corners set
An arbour green, with wandies long and small
Railed about, and so with trees set
Was all the place, and Hawthorne hedges knet,
That lyf was none walking there forbye
That might within scarce any wight espy.
So thick the boughes and the leaves green
Beshaded all the alleys that there were,
And midst of every arbour might be seen
The sharp greene sweet Juniper
Growing so fair with branches here and there,
That as it seemed to a lyf without
The boughes spread the arbour all about
And on the small green twistes sat
The little sweet nightingale, and sung
So loud and clear, the hymn is consecrat
Of loris use, now soft, now loud, among,
That all the gardens and the walles rung
Right of their song.

from
COOPER'S HILL

My eye descending from the Hill, surveys
Where *Thames* amongst the wanton vallies strays.
Thames, the most lov'd of all the Ocean's sons,
By his old Sire to his embraces runs,
Hasting to pay his tribute to the sea,
Like mortal life to meet Eternity.

Sir John Denham

from
ETON BOATING SONG

Jolly boating weather,
And a hay harvest-breeze;
Blade on the feather,
Shade off the trees,
Swing, swing, together,
With your bodies between your knees,
Swing, swing, together
With your bodies between your knees.

Skirling past the rushes,
Ruffling o'er the weeds,
Where the lock-stream gushes,
Where the cygnet feeds,
Let us see how the loving cup flushes,
At supper on Boveney meads,
Let us see how the loving cup flushes
At supper on Boveney meads.

William Johnson Cory

from
ODE ON A DISTANT PROSPECT OF ETON COLLEGE

Ye distant spires, ye antique towers,
That crown the wat'ry glade,
Where grateful Science still adores
Her Henry's holy Shade;
And ye, that from the stately brow
Of Windsor's heights th' expanse below
Of grove, of lawn, of mead survey,
Whose turf, whose shade, whose flowers among
Wanders the hoary Thames along
His silver-winding way.

Ah happy hills, ah pleasing shade,
Ah fields belov'd in vain,
Where once my careless childhood stray'd
A stranger yet to pain!
I feel the gales, that from ye blow,
A momentary bliss bestow,
As waving fresh their gladsome wing,
My weary soul they seem to sooth,
And, redolent of joy and youth,
To breathe a second spring.

Say, Father Thames, for thou hast seen
Full many a sprightly race
Disporting on thy margent green
The paths of pleasure trace,
Who foremost now delight to cleave
With pliant arm thy glassy wave?
The captive linnet which enthrall?
What idle progeny succeed
To chafe the rolling circle's speed,
Or urge the flying ball?

While some on earnest business bent
Their murm'ring labours ply
'Gainst graver hours that bring constraint
To sweeten liberty:
Some bold adventurers disdain
The limits of their little reign,
And unknown regions dare descry:
Still as they run they look behind,
They hear a voice in every wind,
And snatch a fearful joy.

Gay hope is theirs by fancy fed,
Less pleasing when possest;
The tear forgot as soon as shed,
The sunshine of the breast:
Theirs buxom health of rosy hue,
Wild wit, invention ever-new,
And lively chear of vigour born;
The thoughtless day, the easy night,
The spirits pure, the slumbers light,
That fly th' approach of morn.

Alas, regardless of their doom,
The little victims play!
No sense have they of ills to come,
Nor care beyond today:
Yet see how all around 'em wait
The Ministers of human fate,
And black Misfortune's baleful train!
Ah, shew them where in ambush stand
To seize their prey the murth'rous band!
Ah, tell them they are men!

*

To each his suff'rings: all are men,
Condemn'd alike to groan,
The tender for another's pain;
Th' unfeeling for his own.
Yet ah! why should they know their fate?
Since sorrow never comes too late,
And happiness too swiftly flies.
Thought would destroy their paradise.
No more; where ignorance is bliss,
'Tis folly to be wise.

Thomas Gray

from
SLOUGH

Come, friendly bombs, and fall on Slough
It isn't fit for humans now,
There isn't grass to graze a cow
    Swarm over, Death!

Come, bombs, and blow to smithereens
Those air-conditioned, bright canteens,
Tinned fruit, tinned meat, tinned milk, tinned beans
    Tinned minds, tinned breath.

Mess up the mess they call a town -
A house for ninety-seven down
And once a week a half-a-crown
    For twenty years.

          *

Come, friendly bombs, and fall on Slough
To get it ready for the plough.
The cabbages are coming now;
    The earth exhales.

[1937]
                        John Betjeman

COME BACK, SIR JOHN!

Come unfriendly John.   Re-visit Slough.
You'll find it twice as ghastly now,
With concrete structures cheek by jowl,
    Suffocating envelopment.

Come John, and blast with strictures strong,
Those subways with their captive throngs,
The heedless traffic's hideous song,
    The curse of redevelopment.

Expose the mess they call a town,
Gracious houses now pulled down,
For a speculator's greasy pound,
    Lip service to the Green Belt.

And assail those planners, empire building,
Distant, arrogant, and so unheeding,
Of the protests and the pleadings.
    They will not help.

And smash their dreams of future splendour,
As they crush the reluctant vendor,
With purchase orders freely rendered,
    By Whitehall.

But spare the councillors who agree,
Without a question to these mad decrees,
It is not their fault they cannot see.
    They are in thrall.

It's not their fault they cannot know,
That planners run the biggest shows,
So it's not their fault they sometimes go
    To social places.

And talk of loos and abattoirs,
In various bogus sporty bars,
And dream the while of the hurrahs,
    For Mayoral status.

So come Sir John!   Re-visit Slough,
And pledge anew your once-strong vow,
That only falling bombs can now
    Bring merciful hiatus.

[1971]   *John Jones*

33

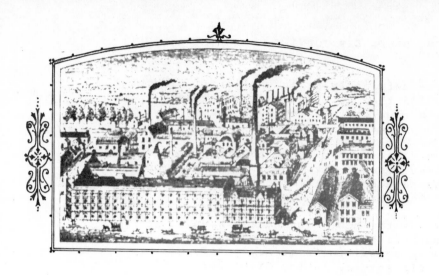

HUNTLEY AND PALMER'S GREAT BISCUIT MANUFACTORY

O! who has not heard of old Reading's famed town,
   So widely made known by the industry there,
Whose goods are sent forth both east, west, south, an
                                  nort
   And with which for quality none can compare.

'Tis built on the banks of old Kennet's fair stream,
   And 'tween it the river doth silently flow;
Neat bridges stretch o'er, thus connecting each shore
   Their useful long arms o'er the waters they throw.

And on either side spacious buildings appear,
   Which cover vast acres of wide stretching space;
With red brick and stone, due proportion is shown,
   And all well arranged in their own proper place.

Tall shafts tow'ring upwards and piercing the sky,
   Like mainmasts that stretch from the deck down bel
Whence borne far away where with clouds it can play,
   The smoke in huge columns doth heavenwards go.

And O! what machinery working within,
   In seeming confusion that puzzles the mind;
How it rattles and hums, its rollers and drums
   And slow trav'lling ovens that evermore wind.

Long straps straight or twisted on wheels large and
                                small,
   All which go one way when the straps travel straig
But when they are changed and inversely arranged
   The wheels are reversed with bewildering rate.

The thud of the "cutters", the roll of the cogs,
    The creak and the whizz of the straps as they fly;
While long sheets of dough up the canvas now go
    All spotless and pure from the "rollers" close by.

No firm equal to it old England can boast,
    Nor indeed can the world its rival e'er show;
Where biscuits and cakes of all sizes and makes
    Impregnate the air with the odours they throw.

Of cakes there are Bristol, Madeira and Lunch,
    The Reading, the Currant, the Plain and the Seed;
Fruit, Almond and Rice, Banquet, Diet and Ice,
    All which are of excellent flavour indeed.

Sultana, Sponge, Wedding, Queen's Heart, Battenburg,
    Genoa, Lucerne, Eton, Orange and Snow;
Milan, Cocoanut (for the palace or hut),
    Sandringham, Lisbon, Cambridge, Rugby also.

Chatsworth and Valencia and Lemon as well,
    Teacakes, Tops and Bottoms and others unknown,
Whose virtues are such connoisseurs praise them much
    At home and abroad in each wide spreading zone.

The names of the biscuits, suffice it to say,
    (They also are nourishing, wholesome and good)
Shall here "legion" be; o'er each far distant sea
    Their merits are known as an excellent food.

                            *

Thus, then, this large firm all earth's races supply
    With Albert, with Brighton, with Bath and Cheapside
Fancy Rout, Macaroon and the sweet Demi Lune
    And dear Littlefolk and the Household beside.

Jamaica, Pearl, Button Nuts, Honey Drops,
    Maziena, Empire, Combination and Queen;
Milk, Camp, Ratafias, Captain, Cuddy and Cheese,
    Rich Travellers, Riviera, Picnic, Madeline.

Nonpareil, German Rusks and Caricature,
    Digestive, Colonial, Nonsuch and Savoy;
Filbert, Diadem, and the neat little Gem,
    Snowflake, Smyrna, Social, Swiss, Toast, Cracknell
                                            Toy.

Caprice, Abernethy, Tea Rusks, Almond Rings,
   Brown College, Meat Wafers and Ice Wafers too;
Walnut, Arrowroot, Universal and Fruit,
   Thin Captain, Presburg, all most sweet, fresh and
                                               new.

Salt, Sicily Nuts, Water, Wheaten, Wheatmeal,
   Nic Nac, Kinder Garten, the Oaten and Roll;
Moss, Tourist, Bodour, and a vast number more,
   I here have but mentioned a half of the whole.

All honour to those who by toil have thus raised
   So useful a monument to their own worth;
Preserving their name and recording their fame
   Which already reaches the ends of the earth.

                        *

                                    J. Mosdell

from
THE BALLAD OF READING GAOL

In Reading gaol by Reading town
   There is a pit of shame,
And in it lies a wretched man
   Eaten by teeth of flame,
In a burning winding-sheet he lies,
   And his grave has got no name.

And there, till Christ call forth the dead,
   In silence let him lie;
No need to waste the foolish tear,
   Or heave the windy sigh:
The man had killed the thing he loved,
   And so he had to die.

And all men kill the thing they love,
   By all let this be heard,
Some do it with a bitter look,
   Some with a flattering word,
The coward does it with a kiss,
   The brave man with a sword!

                        Oscar Wilde

SPEENHAMLAND

[Lines written by a traveller on the windows
of the George and Pelican coaching inn]

The famous inn at Speenhamland
That stands below the hill,
May well be called the Pelican
From its enormous bill.

from
THE LAZY MINSTREL

Bisham

O Bisham Banks are fresh and fair,
And Quary woods are green;
And pure and sparkling is the air,
Enchanting is the scene.

Pangbourne

O Pangbourne is pleasant in sweet summertime,
And Streatley and Goring are worthy of rhyme;
The sunshine is hot and the breezes are still,
The river runs swift under Basildon Hill.

Streatley

But from the hill I understand
You gaze across rich pasture-land,
And fancy you see Oxford and
    P'raps Wallingford and Wheatley;
And, though the view's beyond all praize,
I'd rather much sit here and laze
    Than scale the hill at Streatley.

John Ashby Sterry

THE VICAR OF BRAY

In good King Charles's golden days,
    When loyalty no harm meant;
A furious High Church man I was,
    And so I gained preferment.
Unto my flock I daily preached,
    "Kings are by God appointed,
And damned are those who dare resist,
    Or touch the Lord's Anointed."

And this is Law, I will maintain
    Unto my dying day, Sir,
That whatsoever King shall reign,
    I will be Vicar of Bray, Sir!

When royal James possessed the Crown,
    And Popery grew in fashion,
The Penal Law I hooted down,
    And read the Declaration:
The Church of Rome I found would fit
    Full well my constitution,
And I had been a Jesuit
    But for the Revolution.

And this is Law, etc.

When William our Deliverer came
    To heal the Nation's grievance,
I turned the cat in pan again,
    And swore to him allegiance:
Old principles I did revoke,
    Set Conscience at a distance,
Passive Obedience is a joke,
    A jest is Non-Resistance.

And this is Law, etc.

When glorious Anne became our Queen,
    The Church of England's glory,
Another face of things was seen,
    And I became a Tory:
Occasional Conformists base
    I damned, and Moderation,
And thought the Church in danger was
    From such prevarication.

And this is Law, etc.

When George in pudding time came o'er,
    And moderate men looked big, Sir,
My principles I changed once more,
    And so became a Whig, Sir:
And thus preferment I procured
    From our Faith's Great Defender,
And almost every day abjured
    The Pope and the Pretender.

And this is Law, etc.

The illustrious House of Hanover,
    And Protestant Succession,
To these I lustily will swear,
    Whilst they can keep possession:
For in my Faith and Loyalty
    I never once will falter,
But George my lawful King shall be,
    Except the times should alter.

And this is Law, etc.

Anon.

THE ALBERT MEMORIAL, ABINGDON

*[from an Ode commemorating its
 inauguration, 22nd June 1865]*

This our memorial we gladly rear
To one whose name to us is ever dear;
And round the pile thus built with willing hand
The people of the Royal County stand:
Proud such a hero for their own to claim,
They raise their monument to Albert's fame.

W. Blake Atkinson

APPLETON BELL-RINGERS

[Newspaper advertisement for A.White and Sons, Besselsleigh, near Abingdon, July 1867]

A.White and Sons Belhangers were made,
  Because it was their fancy trade;
In hanging bells they take delight
  To make them go with all their might.
They in their brasses don't confine them,
  Or else no man could ever rise them.
In clappering they're quite expert,
  For in the bell they put the work
That makes the clapper to rebound,
  Which brings the true and proper sound.
In tuning they are competent,
  To tuning fork, and instrument.
In ringing bells also they're right,
  For they're a band whose name is WHITE:
They'll ring their bells with any band,
  To Treble Bob, Grandsire, or Stedman;
Hand Bells they make; are skill'd in tuning,
  Can ring some tunes that are amusing;
If you've a peal that's not quite right,
  Just drop a line to ALFRED WHITE,
And with his SONS he will come down,
  Re-hang the bells, and make them sound
The proper note, that's not been heard
  Perhaps for as much as twenty years.
His SONS the clocks and chimes can do,
  Make them play tunes and keep time true.
If you've a job that's worth attention,
  They will do their best to give satisfaction.

from
UPPER LAMBOURNE

Leathery limbs of Upper Lambourne,
    Leathery skin from sun and wind,
Leathery breeches, spreading stables,
    Shining saddles left behind,
To the down the string of horses
    Moving out of sight and mind.

Feathery ash in leathery Lambourne
    Waves above the sarsen stone,
And Edwardian plantations
    So coniferously moan
As to make the swelling downland,
    Far surrounding, seem their own.

John   Betjeman

ILSLEY

[traditional rhymes]

Ilsley, remote amidst the Berkshire downs,
Claims these distinctions o'er her sister towns;
Far famed for sheep and wool, though not for spinners,
For sportsmen, doctors, publicans and sinners!

Sleepy Ilsley, drunken people,
Got a church without a steeple;
And what is more, to their disgrace,
They've got a clock without a face!

from
A DAY ON THE DOWNS

The Ridgeway Road

Hence come we to the Ridgeway Road;
It's straight, it's green, and it is broad.
(When master here proud Rome became,
Then Ik'neld, Hick'rel, was its name.)
Here ancient Britons moved along,
With flocks and herds, a numerous throng.
When Albion felt her first alarms,
And first beheld the Roman arms,
This way they fled, and with them bore
Their all, for safety, from the shore.

The Seven Barrows

From hence, along the eastern border,
See seven mounds arise in order.
Cairns and cromlechs, rear'd with stones,
Of old contain'd distinguish'd bones,
        But here were bodies burn'd.
Here once was a Gehenna dire,
Of mortal flesh consumed with fire!
What nauseous odours must have been,
What horrid customs here were seen,
        When dead men's dust was urn'd!
And fragments found may plainly show,
Of arrows, vases, spear, and bow,
That Britons, Romans, Saxons, Danes,
Who figured once along the plains,
        In low confusion lie.
The largest giants earth has bred,
The great who fear and terror spread,
        What are they when they die?

The Blow Stone
or, King Alfred's Bugle

This stone, which utter'd many a blast,
In silence lay for ages past.
By man unheard, by man unseen,
Tradition said it once had been,
And that for miles its loud alarms
Were heard when Alfred blew to arms.
And this tradition had it still,
The stone was on the White Horse Hill.
From sire to son the Blow Stone tale
Thus circled round the White Horse Vale.

Francis Rose

LOLLINGDON DOWNS

Up on the downs the red-eyed kestrels hover,
Eyeing the grass.
The field-mouse flits like a shadow into cover
As their shadows pass.

Men are burning the gorse on the down's shoulder;
A drift of smoke
Glitters with fire and hangs, and the skies smoulder,
And the lungs choke.

Once the tribe did thus on the downs, on these downs,
                                        burning
Men in the frame,
Crying to the gods of the downs till their brains were
                                        turning
And the gods came.

And today on the downs, in the wind, the hawks, the
                                        grasses,
In blood and air,
Something passes me and cries as it passes,
On the chalk downland bare.

John Masefield

43

from
THE BALLAD OF THE WHITE HORSE

Before the gods that made the gods
   Had seen their sunrise pass,
The White Horse of the White Horse Vale
   Was cut out of the grass.

Before the gods that made the gods
   Had drunk at dawn their fill,
The White Horse of the White Horse Vale
   Was hoary on the hill.

                    G.K. Chesterton

THE SCOURING OF THE WHITE HORSE

[ancient ballad]

The owld White Harse wants zettin' to rights
And the Squire hev promised good cheer,
Zo we'll gee un a scrape to kip un in zhape
And a'll last for many a year.

CHARGED LANDSCAPE: UFFINGTON

From the eye of the Uffington White Horse
the downs' every feature.   Spur, combe
and fluting;   lifted by low sun

waves of a fossil sea, surging again
as wind through barley, breaking
on Berkshire's plain.   The hand of man

who cleared scrub - yew and juniper;   felled
trees below, exposing to view this land's
form, kept cropped by sheep and cultivation.

Cut through turf then, to this sea-horse,
tip of a contour's whip uncoiling,
crack of it - hooves' strike on storm's iron? -

lightning, will loose on earth rain.
At night, the white chalk reflecting, become
moon in the form, mare;   fecund

to the sun her stallion.   Who depended
for life on these things, each year
came as grooms to her, with hands scarred

by labour scouring flanks of the hill
until, the work done, made celebration in
the scooped hollow its earthen castle.

Come now, from close-to join up
detail to detail, bold
curve of back or foreleg, to an imagined

whole;   and, from this eye, look to
the horizon, Harwell's shimmering:
charged with the same power that's here?

Philip Pacey

from
THE RETURN

From Andover to Wantage Town
Is nigh on forty mile:
You go all day on a grassy way
With not a stone nor stile,
And some companionable wind
Speaks to you all the while.

You are so high above the world,
That, as the shepherd tells,
When the wind blows up from South and West
It brings the sharp sea-smells;
And elfin-dim when the North wind blows,
You hear the Oxford bells.

It is I that would hear the Oxford bells
Above the Oxford flowers,
When the chestnuts are a-droop with drouth,
Sounding the sleepy hours;
Or quavering in the loud March gale
That thunders round her towers.

It is I that am fain to walk again
Where the smooth downs curve and rise;
Where the voices of men are deep and kind,
And the lads have faithful eyes;
And noble in its loneliness
The ancient Ridgeway lies.

St John Lucas

Oxfordshire

THAMES AND ISIS

The famous River Isis hath her spring
Neare Tetbury and downe along doth bring
(As hand-maids) to attend her progress, Churne,
Colne, Windrush, Yenload, Leech, whose windings turne
And Meads and Pastures trims, bedecks and dresses,
Like an unvaluable chaine of Esses.
After releese of many a Ducke and Goose,
At Saint John's Bridge they make their rendevous,
And there like robbers crossing London way,
Bid many a barefoot Welshman wade or stay,
Close under Oxford, one of England's eyes,
Chief of the chiefest Universities.
From Banbury, desirous to add knowledge
To zeal, and to be taught in Magdalen College,
The River Cherwell doth to Isis runne
And bears her company to Abington.

[1632]   *John Taylor*

from
THE SCHOLAR GIPSY

For most, I know, thou lov'st retired ground.
   Thee, at the ferry, Oxford riders blithe,
    Returning home on summer nights, have met
   Crossing the stripling Thames at Bab-lock-hythe,
   Trailing in the cool stream thy fingers wet,
     As the slow punt swings round:
And leaning backward in a pensive dream,
  And fostering in thy lap a heap of flowers
  Pluck'd in shy fields and distant Wychwood bowers,
And thine eyes resting on the moonlit stream.

And then they land, and thou art seen no more.
   Maidens, who from the distant hamlets come
    To dance around the Fyfield elm in May,
  Oft through the darkening fields have seen thee roam,
   Or cross a stile into the public way.
    Oft thou hast given them store
Of flowers - the frail-leaf'd, white anemone -
  Dark bluebells drench'd with dews of summer eves -
  And purple orchises with spotted leaves -
But none has words she can report of thee.

And, above Godstow Bridge, when hay-time's here
   In June, and many a scythe in sunshine flames,
   Men who through those wide fields of breezy grass
  Where black-winged swallows haunt the glittering Thames,
   To bathe in the abandon'd lasher pass,
    Have often pass'd thee near
Sitting upon the river bank o'ergrown:
  Mark'd thine outlandish garb, thy figure spare,
  Thy dark vague eyes, and soft abstracted air;
But, when they come from bathing, thou wert gone.

At some lone homestead in the Cumner hills,
   Where at her open door the housewife darns,
   Thou hast been seen, or hanging on a gate
  To watch the threshers in the mossy barns.
   Children, who early range these slopes and late
    For cresses from the rills,
Have known thee watching, all an April day,
  The springing pastures and the feeding kine;
And mark'd thee, when the stars come out and shine,
Through the long dewy grass move slow away.

In autumn, on the skirts of Bagley Wood,
   Where most the Gipsies by the turf-edg'd way
    Pitch their smok'd tents, and every bush you see
   With scarlet patches tagg'd and shreds of grey,
    Above the forest ground called Thessaly -
      The blackbird picking food
   Sees thee, nor stops his meal, nor fears at all;
    So often has he known thee past him stray,
    Rapt, twirling in thy hand a wither'd spray,
And waiting for the spark from Heaven to fall.

Matthew Arnold

from
ON WESTWALL DOWNES

When Westwall Downes I gan to tread,
Where cleanely wynds the greene did sweepe,
Methought a landskipp there was spread,
Here a bush and there a sheepe:
   The pleated wrinkles of the face
   Of wave-swolne earth did lend such grace,
   As shadowings in Imag'ry
   Which both deceive and please the eye.

         *

Here and there twoe hilly crests
Amiddst them hugg a pleasant greene,
And these are like twoe swelling breasts
That close a tender fall betweene.
   Here would I sleepe, or read, or pray
   From early morn till flight of day:
   But harke! a sheepe-bell calls mee upp,
   Like Oxford colledge-bells, to supp.

William Strode

THE STRIPLING THAMES

As I came down from Bablock-Hythe
Through meads yet virgin of the scythe,
The air was sweet, the birds were blithe
    Along the stream to Eynsham.

The guelder-bloom and flower o' May,
And marguerites and elder spray,
Made either bank a milky way
    From Bablock-Hythe to Eynsham.

Fast anchored 'neath the wild-rose bowers,
Like lovely thoughts transformed to flowers,
The lilies dreamed away the hours
    'Twixt Bablock-Hythe and Eynsham;

And youthful yet, and lately bound
On his adventure, he has found
Our pilgrim Thames, his holy ground
    From Bablock-Hythe to Eynsham.

How can he know, the while he threads
His silver course through golden meads,
The angry wave to which he leads,
    At last, at last, from Eynsham?

Sun and sweet air, - the harmony
Of earth and June! It seemed to me
A dream of all that youth should be,
    My waterway to Eynsham.

But ah, how brief the magic spell!
True type of youth; bright streams, farewell.
Alas! we cannot always dwell
    'Twixt Bablock-Hythe and Eynsham.

St John Lucas

from
THYRSIS

How changed is here each spot man makes or fills!
  In the two Hinkseys nothing keeps the same;
    The village street its haunted mansion lacks,
  And from the sign is gone Sibylla's name,
    And from the roofs the twisted chimney-stacks -
      Are ye too changed, ye hills?
  See, 'tis no foot of unfamiliar men
    Tonight from Oxford up your pathway strays!
    Here came I often, often, in old days -
  Thyrsis and I; we still had Thyrsis then.

Runs it not here, the track from Childsworth Farm,
  Past the high wood, to where the elm tree crowns
    The hill behind whose ridge the sunset flames?
  The signal-elm, that looks on Ilsley Downs,
    The Vale, the three lone weirs, the youthful
                                      Thames?
    This winter-eve is warm,
Humid the air! leafless, yet soft as spring,
  The tender purple spray on copse and briers!
  And that sweet city with her dreaming spires,
She needs not June for beauty's heightening.

                          Matthew Arnold

from
THE CHERWELL

O many an evening have I been
Entranced upon that glorious scene,
When silent thought hath proved too strong
For utterance in tranquil song.
There intermingling with the trees
The city rose in terraces
Of radiant buildings, backed with towers
And dusky folds of elm-tree bowers.
St Mary's watchmen, mute and old,
Each rooted in a buttress bold,
From out their lofty niche looked down
Upon the calm monastic town,
Upon the single glistering dome,
And princely Wykeham's convent home,
And the twin minarets that spring
Like buoyant arrows taking wing,
And square in Moorish fashion wrought
As though from old Granada brought,
And that famed street, whose goodly show
In double crescent lies below,
And Bodley's court and chestnut bower
  That overhangs the garden wall,
And sheds all day white flakes of flower
  From off its quiet coronal.
Methinks I see it at this hour,
  How silently the blossoms fall.

F.W. Faber

AT OXFORD

Though cold December rains draw vanishing rings
  On the choked Isis that goes swirling by,
These academic gowns flap like the wings
  Of half-fledged blackbirds that attempt to fly.

Andrew Young

from
DEDICATORY ODE

Can this be Oxford? This the place?
  (He cries) Of which my father said
The tutoring was a damned disgrace,
  The Creed a mummery stuffed and dead?

Can it be here that Uncle Paul
  Was driven by excessive gloom
To drink and debt, and, last of all
  To smoking opium in his room?

Is it from here the people come,
  Who talk so loud, and roll their eyes
And stammer? How extremely rum!
  How curious! What a great surprise!

                    Hilaire Belloc

from
ALMA MATER

Know you her secret, none can utter?
  Hers of the Book, the tripled Crown?
Still on the spire the pigeons flutter,
  Still by the gateway flits the gown;
Still on the street, from corbel and gutter,
  Faces of stone look down.

Faces of stone, and stonier faces -
  Some from library windows wan
Forth on her gardens, her green spaces,
  Peer and turn to their books anon.
Hence, my Muse, from the green oases
  Gather the tent, begone!

                    A. Quiller-Couch

from
CANTERBURY TALES
[Prologue]

The Clerk of Oxford

A CLERK ther was of Oxenford also,
That un-to logik hadde long y-go.
As lene was his hors as is a rake,
And he nas nat right fat, I undertake;
But loked holwe, and ther-to soberly.
Ful thredbar was his overest courtepy;
For he had geten him yet no benefyce,
Ne was so worldly for to have offyce.
For him was lever have at his beddes heed
Twenty bokes, clad in blak or reed,
Of Aristotle and his philosophye,
Than robes riche, or fithele, or gay sautrye.
But al be that he was a philosophre,
Yet hadde he but litel gold in cofre;
But al that he mighte of his freendes hente,
On bokes and on lerninge he it spente,
And bisily gan for the soules preye
Of hem that gaf him wher-with to scoleye.
Of studie took he most cure and most hede.
Noght o word spak he more than was nede,
And that was seyd in forme and reverence,
And short and quik, and ful of hy sentence.
Souning in moral vertu was his speche,
And gladly wolde he lerne, and gladly teche.

Geoffrey Chaucer

ON OXFORD

The Gothic looks solemn,
   The plain Doric column
Supports an old Bishop and Crosier;
   The mouldering arch
   Shaded o'er by a larch
Stands next door to Wilson the Hosier.

Vicè - that is, by turns, -
   O'er pale faces mourns
The black tassell'd trencher and common hat;
   The Chantry boy sings,
   The Steeple-bell rings,
And as for the Chancellor - *dominat.*

There are plenty of trees,
   And plenty of ease,
And plenty of fat deer for Parsons;
   And when it is venison,
   Short is the benison, -
Then each on a leg or thigh fastens.

John Keats

FRESHMEN

Scholar-type from Winchester or (sometimes) Eton
Coming up to New Coll. with other pleasant guys,
With luggage full of Berlioz,
Lapsang-Soochong,
Apparatus criticus and neat bow ties.

Mustard-keen commoner from Midland grammar school,
Never letting on he doesn't know the ropes,
With luggage full of Sullivan,
Penguins, County Grants,
Sherry glasses, marmalade and microscopes.

Muscle-man from Empire with dirt-caked sports shorts,
Butting through the Trials to a Rugger Blue,
With luggage full of Tiger Rag,
Food stuffs, track suits,
Liniments, boots, and a book, or two.

Maida Stanier

CHRIST CHURCH BELLS

O! the bonny Christ Church Bells
One, two, three, four, five six,
That ring so mighty sweet,
So wonderous great,
And trowle so merrily, merrily.

O the first and second Bell,
Which every day at four and ten
Cry come, come, come, come, come,
Come to prayers,
And ye verger troops before ye Deane.

Tingle, tingle, tingle
Says the little bell att 9
To call the beerers home;
But the devill a man
Will leave his Can
Till hee hears the mighty Tome.

[c.1670]   *Thomas Baskerville*

THE MARRIED EX-FELLOW'S REGRETS

Why did I sell my college life
(He cries) for benefice and wife?
Return, ye days, when endless pleasure
I found in reading, or in leisure!
When calm around the common-room
I puffed my daily pipe's perfume!
Rode for a stomach and inspected,
At annual bottlings, corks selected,
And dined untaxed, untroubled under
The portrait of our pious Founder!
When impositions were supplied
To light my pipe - or soothe my pride -
No cares were then for forward peas,
A yearly-longing wife to please;
My thoughts no christening-dinners crossed
No children cried for buttered toast!
And every night I went to bed
Without a Modus in my head!

T. Warton

CHRIST CHURCH, OXFORD

Night

Faint from the bell the ghastly echoes fall,
  That grates within the grey cathedral tower;
Let me not enter through the portal tall,
  Lest the strange spirit of the moonless hour
Should give a life to those pale people, who
Lie in their fretted niches, two and two -
Each with his head on pillowy stone reposed,
And his hands lifted, and his eyelids closed.

A cold and starless vapour, through the night,
  Moves as the paleness of corruption passes
Over a corpse's features, like a light
  That half illumines what it most effaces;
The calm round water gazes on the sky,
Like the reflection of the lifeless eye
Of one who sleeps and dreams of being slain,
Struggling in frozen frenzy, and in vain.

From many a mouldering oriel, as to flout
  Its pale, grave brow of ivy-tressèd stone,
Comes the incongruous laugh, and revel shout:-
  Above, some solitary casement, thrown
Wide open to the wavering night wind,
Admits its chill - so deathful, yet so kind
Unto the fevered brow and fiery eye
Of one, whose night hour passeth sleeplessly.

Ye melancholy chambers! I could shun
  The darkness of your silence, with such fear,
As places where slow murder had been done.
  How many noble spirits have died here,
Withering away in yearnings to aspire,
Gnawed by mocked hope - devoured by their own fire!
Methinks the grave must feel a colder bed
To spirits such as these, than unto common dead.

John Ruskin

OXFORDSHIRE

traditional rhymes

Aynho on the hill,
Clifton in the clay,
Drunken Deddington
And Yam highway.

I went to Noke,
And nobody spoke,
I went to Brill,
They were silent still,
I went to Thame,
It was just the same,
I went to Beckley,
They spoke directly.

Hayley, Crawley, Curbridge and Coggs,
Witney spinners and Ducklington dogs,
Finstock on the hill, Fawler down derry,
Beggarly Ramsden, and lousy Charlbury,
Woodstock for bacon, Bladon for beef,
Hanborough for a scurvy knave,
And Combe for a thief.

*Marsh Baldon, Toot Baldon, Baldon-on-the-Green,
Big Baldon, Little Baldon and Baldon in between.*

ODE TO THE MONTHLY MEETING
Islip Women's Institute

*Village Hall
  Small rent
Two hours
  Well spent*

*Lecture good
  Rather funny
Tea next
  Empty tummy*

*Jerusalem sung
  Record signed
Business done
  Correctly timed*

*Produce stall
  Nice sum
Sold out
  Well done*

Grace Henman

BANBURY CROSS

There were ten Otter-hunters for sport at a loss,
So they met in October at Banbury Cross;
They longed for the horn, with its ravishing sound,
So the music they tried of the true basset-hound.

Chorus:

> *Ride a Cock-horse to Banbury Cross*
> *To see a fine lady ride on a white horse;*
> *Rings on her fingers, and bells on her toes;*
> *Oh! she shall have music wherever she goes.*

So these ten Otter-hunters full early set forth
To the meet of the basset-hounds run by Lord North;
They found a stout hare, and they ran her all day,
And they killed her at Broughton, some five miles away.

Then to the White Lion by Banbury Cross
They footed it, not having any Cock-horse;
They emptied the larder, they drank all the beer,
Till host Page for the next morning's breakfast
    did fear.

Then with bells on their fingers and pumps on their
    toes,
They make music and song till the morning cock crows;
And the songs that they sing, as a matter of course,
Are about the fine lady of Banbury Cross.

Of these ten Otter-hunters the names would you know?
There were two little Metters, and Turralls also;
There were Vernons and Munros, Macdonald and Lowe,
Rupert Uthwatt, Cattell, and the rest I don't know.

Arthur MacDonald

THOUGHTS FROM THE HILL ABOVE ISLIP BRIDGE

The seven towns of Otmoor lie silent in the plain,
Oddington, Merton, Charlton,
Fencot, Murcot, Beckley, Noke.
A tower glows red agin the setting sun,
Slate roofs and thatch of Islip's town.
A town famed in history since the Confessor's reign.

What spirits haunt this countryside on All Hallows
E'en?
John of Islip, Buckland, South,
John Buchan, Lovelace, Cromwell?
A horseman straining at his horse's mouth
To find a phantom hunt in Noke?
Hounds are heard, and tally-ho, yet nought is seen.

These spirits pass, and there comes a crowd of merry
boys,
South's schoolboys, clad in Blue Coat gear,
Followed close by a weird form
'Tis Tiglath Pileser, Frank Buckland's bear
Who plods contently round the roads,
Frights the folk, and raids the shops for treacle,
sweets and toys.

A changed scene now, the Book of Time has turned
another page,
Armies camp on Bicester hill,
Otmoor now a bombing range.
A traveller pauses on his way to Brill.
What think you of the future, friend,
Does the world now look forward to an atomic age?

G.H. Blanchett

from
SPRING

   Hark! hark! the wakeful lark's harmonious lay,
With outstretch'd wing salutes the op'ning day:
While from the woods the wild-note thrushes sing;
The tuneful blackbird's joy proclaims the Spring.
    The Winter gone, the charming Spring is near,
   Welcome thou fairest season of the year.

   Now shoots the cowslip with redoubled pace;
Now fragrant vi'lets humble bushes grace;
Now daisy-tufts abound, with primrose pale,
While streaked tulips curious eyes regale;
    Narcissus fair, and delicate jonquil,
   And woodbine sweet, the air with odours fill.

   See where the little Glyme delightsome flows,
And to the meads its fertile sweets disclose.
Upon her banks the charming nightingale
Fills with her warbling notes the flow'ry vale.
While all the other chanters are at rest,
What lovely strains arises from her breast.
    Sweetly she sings until the dawn appear,
   Rejoicing in this season of the year.

                           John Bennet

from
WOODSTOCK: AN ELEGY

O Woodstock, fated long to be the seat
   Of all the charms that wit and beauty boast,
The hero's guerdon, and his soft retreat,
   Yielding content, in fields and senates lost.

Thy glories now are level'd low in earth;
   No longer beauty doth thy bow'rs adorn;
No more thy woods resound the voice of mirth;
   The laurel from thy victor brow is torn!

                       Hugh Dalrymple

WOODSTOCK PALACE

*[Lines written in charcoal on the
window-shutter of the room where the
future Queen Elizabeth I was imprisoned
by her sister Mary Tudor]*

Oh! Fortune! how thy restlesse wavering state
   Hath fraught with cares my troubled witt
Witness this present Prisonn whither fate
   Could beare me and the joys I quit.
Thou causedst the guiltie to be losed
From bandes wherein are innocents inclosed
Causing the guiltles to be straites reserved
And freeing those that Death well deserved
But by her envy can be nothing wroughte
So God send to my foes all they have thoughte.

A.D. 1555   *Elizabethe Prisoner*

BLENHEIM PALACE

See, sir, here's the grand approach;
This way for his Grace's coach:
There lies the bridge, and here's the clock,
Observe the lion and the cock,
The spacious court, the colonnade,
And mark how wide the hall is made!
The chimneys are so well design'd,
They never smoke in any wind.
This gallery's contrived for walking,
The windows to retire and talk in;
The council chamber for debate,
And all the rest are rooms of state.

   Thanks, sir, cried I, 'tis very fine,
But where d'ye sleep, or where d'ye dine?
I find, by all you have been telling,
That 'tis a house, but not a dwelling.

Alexander Pope

62

from
BLENHEIM

   Those scenes are vanish'd - scarce a trace remains,
And scarce one vestige Nature's face retains.
Oblivion broods upon the levell'd lawn,
And fly the tints by History's pencil drawn.
The turf-grown Palace shews no antique tower;
Nor wail the Loves in ROSAMONDA's Bower:
A SPRING alone preserves her ill-starr'd name,
Recals her beauty, and confirms her shame;
Thus ARETHUSA rolls recording waves,
And AGANIPPE's fount her memory saves.
   But let not Fancy mourn, or Genius weep,
Though ancient scenes are sunk in iron sleep;
Though ALBION's kings relinquish WOODSTOCK's shades,
Her flowery vallies, and her airy glades;
With raptur'd eye, see stately BLENHEIM rise,
And lift sublime her turrets to the skies.
Imperial BLENHEIM! in whose ample round,
United strength and majesty are found;
Vast in design, with every beauty grac'd,
That strikes the sense, and charms the eye of taste:
At once the monument of arms and arts,
The Hero's meed, the pledge of BRITISH hearts;
Till Time's remotest stage, design'd to prove,
A CHURCHILL's valour, and a Nation's love.

W. Mavor

KELMSCOTT
[lines written for an embroidered bed-hanging]

The wind's on the wold
And the night is a-cold,
And Thames runs chill
'Twixt mead and hill.
But kind and dear
Is the old house here
And my heart is warm
'Midst winter's harm.
Rest then and rest,
And think of the best
'Twixt summer and spring,
When all birds sing
In the town of the tree,
And ye lie in me
And scarce dare move,
Lest earth and its love
Should fade away
Ere the full of the day.
I am old and have seen
Many things that have been;
Both grief and peace
And wane and increase.
No tale I tell
Of ill or well,
But this I say:
Night treadeth on day,
And for worst or best
Right good is rest.

William Morris

The Poets

Matthew Arnold (1822-1888)

W.B. Atkinson (fl.1867-1899)

Thomas Baskerville (1630-1720)

Hilaire Belloc (1870-1953)

John Bennet (fl.1774-1796)
a journeyman shoemaker of Woodstock

John Betjeman (C20)

Geraldine H. Blanchett (C20)

Stanley Brandon (C20)

Geoffrey Chaucer (1340-1400)

Hugh Chesterman (C20)

G.K. Chesterton (1874-1936)

W.J. Cory (1823-1892)

William Cowper (1731-1800)

Hugh Dalrymple (d.1774)

Sir John Denham (1615-1669)

Michael Drayton (1563-1631)

Queen Elizabeth I (r.1558-1603)

F.W. Faber (1814-1863)

Thomas Gray (1716-1771)

Grace Henman (C20)

H. Evelyn Howard (1900-1941)

King James I of Scotland (r.1406-1437)

John Jones (C20)

John Keats (1795-1821)

William Lane (fl.1792-1856)
a poor labouring man of Flackwell Heath

St John Lucas (1879-1934)

Sylvia Lynd (C20)

Arthur MacDonald (C20)

John Masefield (1878-1967)

William Mavor (1758-1837)

William Morris (1834-1896)

J. Mosdell (C19)

Philip Pacey (C20)

Thomas Love Peacock (1785-1866)

A. Quiller-Couch (1863-1944)

Eva N. Rolls (C20)

Theodora Roscoe (C20)

Francis Rose (C19)

John Ruskin (1819-1900)

John Schorn (C15)

B. Seeley (C18)
a bookseller of Buckingham

Percy Bysshe Shelley (1792-1822)

Edmund Spenser (1552-1599)

Maida Stanier (C20)

John Ashby Sterry (fl.1870-1913)

William Strode (1602-1645)

John Taylor (1580-1653)

James Thomson (1700-1748)

W.T. Thorpe (C20)

Cartwright Timms (C20)

William Tyler (C19)

Thomas Warton (1728-1790)

Charles Whitehall (C19)
a gardener of Gawscott

Oscar Wilde (1854-1900)

Thomas Wright (C20)

Andrew Young (1885-1971)

POET'S ENGLAND

To assist in the compilation of this
series the publishers would be glad to
hear from libraries with local collections
of verse and from regional poets who
would like their work to be considered
for inclusion in future volumes.

Also from Brentham Press

THE BEAUTY OF LIFE by William Morris
Abridged from an address given in Birmingham in
1880, first published as "Labour and pleasure versus
labour and sorrow". Printed brown on cream, Morris-
style cover design.
24 pages   ISBN 0 9503459 0 3   40 pence

ON MODERN GARDENING by Horace Walpole
Written in 1770, Walpole's classic essay on the
development of landscape gardening starts in Eden
and finishes with Capability Brown. Reprinted green
on cream, line drawings by Jane Dawnay.
32 pages   ISBN 0 9503459 2 X   50 pence

AND ALSO MUCH CATTLE by D. S. Savage
Scenario for four male voices, in verse.
A negro version of Jonah and the Whale, originally
broadcast on BBC Third Programme with music by
Christopher Whelen. Especially suitable for church
and youth groups.
16 pages   ISBN 0 9503459 5 4   30 pence
           (with musical score, £1.00 inc. postage)

Please add postage 10p each title

BRENTHAM PRESS 137 Fowler's Walk London W5

758

DATE DUE FOR RETURN

This book may be recalled before the above date

90014